Entangling

Poems by Peacef Pya

by
Peacef Pya

Zorba Press
Ithaca, New York, USA
www.ZorbaPress.com

ISBN: 9780927379939
Release date: 2017-March-21

The image on the front cover is a reproduction of the fantastic painting "Mind Form 03", by the extaordinary artist, Naoto Hattori. The author and publisher are deeply grateful to Mr. Hattori for his permission to use this image. More of Naoto's work can be seen at his website: www.naotohattori.com

Published by Zorba Press
Ithaca, New York, USA
http://www.ZorbaPress.com

For more information about this book
and its author, contact Zorba Press:
email: books@zorbapress.com

Version: pag009/cov011
Printings: 0203040506070809101112131415161718192

Contents

Entangling

TO MY DAUGHTER

Dearest Daughter,

You were once the best dream I had,
and now you are the sweetest of everything I live ...
how blessed I am to live each and every moment
together with you smiling at the present moment
not as granted but as a priceless gift.

Your Mother

A Promenade

My love for you
is like walking in the streets
next to an elephant
dyed in loud pink.

I must, at this moment, clarify:
this promenade
definitely does not take place
on the streets of India
where such an act
would very well be considered
utterly ordinary.

Since We Last Met

Since we last met
how many birds have made nests on trees?
How many lovers have sat under those trees?
How many words have they spoken?
How many dreams have become real?

Since we last met
how many men have looked in a mirror?
How many women have smiled?
How many times have you smiled?
How many trees have you seen
with birds in and lovers under?
How many times have you thought of me?
How many words have you spoken?
How many of those words were about me?

Realism

By the river where the young wanderer walks
there lies a coin on the mossy ground.
Childishly, the young man grabs the coin
tosses it up in the air.

Now we have three possible endings.

The coin falls down:
heads

The coin falls down:
tails

The coin falls down:
the young wanderer doesn't look down
to see whether it is heads or tails.

Tides Of My Heart

There's a quarrel between the tides of my heart:
Some say "Let's flow wild!"
Others say "Let's sit still!"

Monsoon

All my dreams
are
falling
down.

Awakened by the cold raindrops
I say —
the monsoon of my feelings is yet to come.

Forgive My Enthusiasm

I am
falling down
like a drop of water
towards you
traveling at full speed
at the speed of light
towards you.

I am learning new languages
to write poems in them for you
about
drops of water
speed of light
me and you.

The Third
(A fractal pattern of poetry about lives that intersect.)

The old man entered the old barber shop
looked for his new acquaintance
a greeting first
then a warm Cuban reply.
Some fussing from the old man, the new neighbor on
   the street
about the hardship
of moving in to his son's apartment at an old age.
Then a few self-comforting words
about the joy of living with grandchildren.
Finally, to the old barber, he asked the question —
Who are the other two in this photo on the wall?

Forty years ago
we were three friends
three musicians performing in the streets
in the streets of Havana.
We've been friends since birth
me and the one on my right.
Then came this third
the one on my left.

Could he play the guitar?
Man, could he play!
But I could sing, you know.

Yes, he had his moves while playing the guitar.
Girls loved those moves.

The barber stood up
grabbed the picture frame
and then lifted it from the wall.
He wiped the dusty frame with the right sleeve of his
    shirt
and then gave the picture to his new friend.
Tapping on his young self in the picture, he said —
Look at this face, I was the most handsome
that's why they always made me sit in the middle.

I told my friend
I told him two is always better than three.
But he did not listen to me.

And so
we were three musicians
performing in the streets
me
my best friend
and this third!

Dusk

Something vague but still crystal clear.
Something cold but warm like a beloved.
Such complexity in such simplicity.
I have no earthly adjectives to describe this
I need to invent some new ones.
Until that day
let me wander in solitude.

Nothing can fit in a place that it isn't made for.
I am made of something
not carbon
not iron
not zinc.
I am in a vehicle that you call a human being.
I am not cells, bones, water or body.
I do not breathe, my vehicle does
I am not clay
just my body is.

I am just a being traveling at a very high speed
towards a black hole somewhere in the universe.
I am not matter, then why fear death ?
I am not matter, then why fear black holes ?
I don't bite apples
I don't dance.
However

on a summer dusk
looking at the horizon
there is something there I am made of.
It owns me
I own it.

I recall something
that something reminds me of a glory
worn by a feeling of an exile.
I don't want to cry
I'm not happy, either.
A kind of surrender.
A kind of surrender
in diminishing agony.

In the midst of matter
soil, concrete, oceans, boats, and birds
the soul craves for something
something that is not something
not somebody
or somewhere.

How trapped we are
in the freedom of being human.

Every sunset I set sail
from the land of matter
into a horizon that's pink, red, and purple.
Then a strange homelessness
then a deep homesickness.

Entangling

All believe
every human being
is connected to their mother
with an umbilical cord.

Some believe
every soul
is connected to their body
with a silver cord.

And only a few believe
every soul
is connected to each other
with unseen cords
entangling every second
making us a single entity
a single soul.

This entangling of souls, to me,
is the greatest dance to watch
equally as beautiful as
watching
the colossal dance of the universe.

Collision

The chances that I would meet someone like you
are the same as if
a huge comet or a meteor
hits another space object
somewhere out there in space.

How extraterrestrial that would be
for a terrestrial couple like us
who bumped into each other
in a shopping mall!

In a sensible explanation
our encounter is a coincidence
in pulp fiction
they would call it a twist of fate.

Close Embrace

It's raining.
Why don't you find a rose petal
a red one preferably
suspended in the air
and take shelter under it
until I come
and take you both
the red rose petal and you
in my palm?

So
the red rose petal, you and I
jump one after another from the palm
to this poem
cuddling side by side
you and I
under the red rose petal.

Fig Seed

This night is like a ripe fig
cuddled in a soft yellow-green leaf.

Almost with no flaws
almost with no fear
how beautiful the world is tonight !

An entire picture of this moment
in this garden under fig trees
emerges from my soul
the size of a fig seed
as big as love.

Samsara

The finest seed of all seeds
to be planted on Earth
is a human being.

I see with these eyes of mine only.
What if God sees with the eyes of all ?

What if God looks at a red rose with morning dew
and says —
Really! What would God truly say
looking at a red rose with morning dew ?
What would the rose say ?
What do roses say every morning?

The wind blows.
It touches the feathers of a delicate water bird.
Touching the bird, what does the wind say?
What do water birds say?

A hawk flies up out of the lake
with a silent fish in its claws dripping with water.
What do wild birds say?
What do the silent fish in the hawks' claws say ?
Water drops fall to the ground
on a young, slender daisy.
What do daisies in green meadows say?

Humans get born
they grow up
they survive.

Some die too soon
some live a long life.
What does a birth say?
What does a death say?

A sadhu sees this and thrives.
He contemplates, prays, and meditates.
What do the wise eyes of a sadhu say?
Who is it that looks through every eye?
Who is it that runs in every vein?
Who inspires the hawk to be a beast?
The silent fish to be silent?

Let me sit in the green meadows gazing at a daisy!
Let the sadhu pray!
Let the day be bright!
Let the night be dark!

Let Samsara go on!
Let Samsara whirl and whirl!

Delicacy

A flock of birds migrate every sunset
from my heart to a land unknown
a land that's not yet seen
a land that's not yet painted.

Sometime in the afternoon
a couple of pink flamingos land near a green pond.
Gracefully raising their necks
they take turns drinking water.

How delicate a bird can be, I say.
The villain replies —
Go ask the frog in its gut.

An Indian Monsoon

I'm standing still
under the downpour of an Indian monsoon.
I am barefoot
I am pure love
From head to toe, I am all goodwill.
No regrets can touch me nor any fear.
I am at your door.
Open it dearest! Open the door!

Years have come and gone.
My tears have wiped out my fears.
This love has shaken us to the bones.
The time has come to reveal
a new path for us to follow.
Barefoot, I am at your door
under an Indian monsoon.
You must, my love, open the door!

I am worn
I am torn.
Devastated down to my bones.
This love has maddened my soul.
I am helpless, it tears my chest apart.
I have come to your door
in the downpour of an Indian monsoon.
Open the door now!
Open the door!

How much you worry about such little things in life!
How little you wonder about such big secrets!
How tired you are on such an easy path to walk!
How indifferent you are to such significance!

What a big delusion you are falling into.
You are denying love.
You are denying, my dearest,
the language of God.

Lavender

If only I were
a free stream
like you are
and I would flow deep
and cut through
this neighborhood of vast slums.

I sit by the river, it is soon after dusk.
I am jealous of the grace of this dirty river.
Father!
You should have bought me
fewer books or better yet, a tea party set.

Then
a few dogs
gather by the stream
they howl sadly,
too sadly
their noses pointing at the spot
where the dead body of their friends
hit the water
and sank.

Something deep in me hurts.
My longing for you has become a pack of dogs howling,
which is too sad to listen to.

It's sadder to assume
you cannot even hear it.

After that, a woman
a young beautiful one
with dark eyes, long lashes, full lips
standing by the stream
sheds some tears
for her long gone lover
who married the ugly fat daughter of the grocer
and moved into their house
somewhere downtown.

Having grown up
in a house of oak wardrobes
with lavender sachets
it's not easy for me to grasp
the reasons for such behavior.
I don't mean the dogs' behavior
a dog is a dog everywhere
but a human being?

Not having walked ten miles under rain
to pay one dollar less for a three dollar bus fee
and this goddamn scent of lavender sunken in me.

I'm gazing at a basket
floating on the dirt of the dirty river.
I settle more on my river-watching spot
highly determined to wait.

Suddenly, around midnight
the stream
stands up
like an affectionate plump mother.
She stretches the night
like a blanket
over the dreams of the residents of this slum.

A young beautiful boy has been dreaming of
lavender sachets
in an oak wardrobe
in a house full of books.

Veins And Cords

Veins in the human body
submerged under skin and flesh
carry
blood
the vital fluid
for the body to survive.

Cords suspended
in thin air
around sixty inches
up above your head.

What is it that they carry
flowing within entangling cords of karma
from one being to another?

Controlling Self

My heart is on fire
my head is frozen.
My soul is singing and dancing high above
my body is sitting still on a chair.
I am a stranger to myself, an acquaintance with you
still doing my best to conceal
an immense waterfall plunging into you.

Let Tonight Be A Night With You !

Let tonight be a night with you !
Let there be stars in the sky!
Let this not be a dream!
Let that thing deep in us
not hurt like a blade cut tonight!
Let tonight be a night with you!

If my forehead leans on the window glass
let it be because I am waiting for you!
Then suddenly the head leaves the cold glass
as I see you coming around the corner.

Let your sunny hair move
as you walk along the courtyard!
When I open the door, let your eyes of clouds smile!
Let it be such a night tonight!

Let us walk hand in hand to the backyard!
Let us sit there face to face!
Let us talk and talk and talk
may we also laugh and laugh ?
Let our heads spin from happiness !

This wholehearted devotion
is the way of those who have traded
everything for love.

If I hadn't come here tonight
I would have been an apostate
as my religion is loving you.

These stars are always in me
this house, this courtyard, this backyard.
For once
may you and I
be in them, too!

Two Yellow Plums

I have brought two plums for you
both yellow
both very ripe.

During the journey from the tree to you
I made a few attempts to eat one of the plums
and probably I would have eaten the second one
if I had eaten the first one.
But I haven't eaten either one.

I think
you wouldn't have been unhappy
if I had eaten one or even both
as you did not know
about either in the first place.
I asked myself why I couldn't eat them.

Now you are eating them.
Your mouth
enjoys the honey-sweet juice of the bigger plum
and I feel something warm
pouring down
to my heart.
As I watch you eat the other plum
with great appetite
that warmth enters

the rooms of my heart.
Then this warmth becomes a little bird
which flies out through my lips
and nestles
on the twisted corner of your smile.

Snail

Now that the impossible happens and we make up
I know we haven't ever broken up.
What I mean is
imagine we are so close again
to walk with no slippers in the same room.
One of us is a person who hasn't deleted
any of our photos
The other is a person who has deleted them all
in fear of loneliness.
How in the world will these two people
hold on to love?

I cannot be a good friend to anyone.
I am a person who cannot fulfill her promises.
I am so scared of loneliness
I can even rub out holy pictures.
Mother Mary, hold my hands!
Today, I don't like myself at all.

I want to flee deep deep into my own self.
I am becoming more and more like a snail.
Like Cemal Süreya
I bristle with rage against walls and houses
since they are getting between us.

I no longer know who is writing this poem.
It is a dark time in the day.

It happens on Earth.
Snails are raining on my troubled head
on my shoulders
on my back.

You may like traveling without me
eating without me
crying without me
laughing without me.
However, to me
without you
the entire universe is nothing but an ugly makeshift.
Mother Mary
don't you have the slightest affection for me ?
Hold my hands before it's too late!

A reddish brown sky is giving birth
to thousands of snails.
I wonder how many of them will survive.
Maybe a young man will come soon
and just wash the entire sky with blue.
Thus
who will weep for the snail
which impregnated the sky before it died ?

The pain in me does not even fit in poems.
I want to resurrect the dead poets and ask —
Why did you die and leave me all alone ?

Mother Mary
I have no hopes that you will ever come to me
so I am waiting beside the cactus
hoping that it will bloom.

I am a person who cannot keep her promises.
Someone who knows what needs to be done
but who cannot do it
yet I am not willing to call myself selfish.
In the end, am I not my only friend?

Will I, by writing, pay back my debt
to the ships I could not get on
to the languages I can't speak
to the books I haven't read ?

Time
passes
so slowly.
It is not even evening yet.
Time stops.
The snails, the twister, Mother Mary and I
are suspended still in thin air
as if
we are all captured in a painting by Naoto Hattori
hung on a wall in a gallery I have not yet visited.

As a reply to the ones who ask —
What twister is she mentioning here?
Am I supposed to tell you everything?

Conversation With The River Ganges

I know that once
my soul was washed and blessed in you.
You have been calling me for quite a long time
and I ask —
It was love at first sight, do you remember?

You ask me to listen to you
but I hear
nothing but silence
and you say —
At last you can see me.

You say we have a lot in common.
However, I have some more within:
some greed
some hatred
some pain.
You say —
That's why you walk but I flow.

Grace Of Grief

When the wind blows strong passing over huge
   mountains
all those rocks and soil, flora and animals
caressing pebbles
passing through the beasts' fur
passing through the petals of wild roses
through my hair
I see you.

When the wind blows gently over the lake
that blue surface
fidgeting as if unseen raindrops are falling on it
caressing water birds
blowing towards the desolate shore
and the frail branches of the weeping willow are
   scattered by the wind
I see you.

To walk away holding up the neck of my coat
or to vanish into thin air with such sobriety?

The wind is blowing through the holes in my heart.
The weeping willow and I
we both seem to enjoy the grace of grief.
Is the weeping willow there to inspire me
or am I here to inspire the weeping willow
to get scattered this casually by the wind?

By A Whirling Dervish

You, stranger!
Are you lost?
Are you found?
Are you in?
Are you out?
Are you whirling?
Why not?
The universe is whirling as well.

I am a self out of self.
My one hand stretches to the Beloved
my other hand is on the Earth.
I lose self as I whirl
where I lose self, I find God.

An Urge

Sometimes
I get a feeling
to hold the edge and pull out
the wallpaper downloaded in my heart
where chubby elephants
with great memories
remind each other
not to forget you.

How The Heart Breaks

How the heart breaks
is still a mystery
as it has no bones.
Just some muscle and flesh.

The Birdness Of A Bird

The birdness of a bird
does not come from
two wings
or its perfect aerodynamics.

When there is a sweet gentle breeze from the sea
reminding the bird of its birdness
its feet reject the land
the wings stretch
and the bird
flies
towards
the call of freedom
in the way
answered by its birdness.

Ode To My Childhood

It was so great, so great to be a child!
Not being able to find a sensible explanation
why a murmuration of starlings
all of a sudden
start to dance in hundreds
as if they are
one single huge black kite
swirling magically
in the afternoon sky.
Therefore, taking it as a good sign
for something even more magical yet to come.

Waiting for the street vendor
for his fried sheep chitterlings on Wednesdays.
The pastry guy in the mornings
and the old man who sold
wild pears strung on a thread like a necklace
wandering the streets of the town with his donkey
only once a week and in the autumn only.

Believing that I have become rich
when finding a few coins
having the biggest belly by drinking the most coke
buying chocolate from the main street pâtisserie
eating one half
saving the rest to share later with my elder brother.

The bitter chocolate
sold by the gram
wrapped in aluminum foil
handed down to me from the counter.
Believing that this is the whole world
believing that the whole world is me.

Building a swimming pool from a blue plastic basin
a parachute from a soft plastic bag
making a trap for sparrows from a laundry basket.
What's more
it was great to have a mom as my partner in crime.

Watching the smoke coming out of chimneys
my nose sunk in the window glass.
Contemplating the universe
assigning different shapes and colors to aliens
while gazing at the TV antennas on the rooftops.

Listening to songs in a foreign language
that I couldn't yet understand.
Dancing wearing an evening gown of Mom
like in the black-and-white Hollywood movies
and believing wholeheartedly
that real life is supposed to be the same.

Loving a goldfish in a glass bowl.
Being able to see the oceans
in the pebbles, sand, and shells

on the yellowish green bottom of that bowl.
Wondering why cats climb up to the balcony
and how come they can walk safe and sound
when they fall on the ground
waving their tails happily towards the garbage cans.

When was the time I was the saddest?
Fish getting fried
in a kitchen with an open window.
I'm sure it was fish
since I can still smell the frying fish.
Is that me inside the empty house
or is the empty house inside me?
The house with the kitchen where the fish are frying.
What a weird feeling this is!
As if the fish and I are left alone.
Where have all the others gone ?
Years later I learned that
the mother of my mother had died on that day
and immediately
I
the frying fish
the house
were left behind for the neighbors to take care of
in the correct order of concern to my parents.

When was the time I was the happiest?
Was it when
Mom bought me plastic sandals

the loud pink ones
I had been begging for?
Or was it when I was carrying the shopping bag
potatoes at the bottom
pears on them
tomatoes at the top
next to the genuine leather shoes I had taken off
to put on my new fancy sandals?
My little feet in the loud pink sandals
the latest fashion.
All open, made of cheap plastic.
The heat of the soil I was feeling under my feet
the paving stones hurting my soles from under
the thin bottom of these fantastic sandals.
Why was I so happy?
Mom entered the apartment
I hesitated at the door
trying to decide
whether or not to take off the sandals.
The door swung closed.
The staircases had just been washed.
My feet soaking wet
I reached for the door handle
held it
pushed open the door
leaving behind me
the sour smell of mold and wet floor.
I entered home through the gloomy hallway
if you ever wonder

my feet still in the sandals, latest fashion.

Now
when I look back at my childhood
there is just one question in my mind

When was the first time I stopped
running down the stairs
three sets of stairs, twenty-five steps to each floor
welcoming my dad
hugging and kissing him like crazy?

When was the first time you stopped doing that?

Diminishing Lights

The cold wind hits my face
like a razor blade
cutting into the flesh.

It follows the tunnels in my nose
up to my forehead
through the veins
which are somewhat larger
than capillaries
when I consider the wide area which gets prickled
relatively.

I hold the rope tight.
I look up.
I look at the clear night sky
my feet on the deck of the boat
the boat on the water
all together under the effects of gravity
in full compliance with the laws of nature
on the surface of the Earth
rotating in a universe.

This image of the boat
with its empty mast
and the image of me holding the tense rope
again relatively.

I can't help wondering
if the image we manifest all together
can be listed as a phenomenon
anticipated to have the features of fractals.

Our chances are low I think
compared to a Romanesco broccoli
very low indeed
once again relatively.

The Song

I hear a song playing
with sad lyrics but a cheerful tune.

A young man with a good heart
is trying to make the song heard by a young girl.

That's the way big loves are in small towns.

The world is consuming everything
with the appetite of a ravenous ape.

Humans, who are in the minority
in the hell of apes
miss their beloveds.

Light And Darkness

Slowly, without moving your body
turn your head to darkness.
You can still see some light coming.

Now
turn your head to the light.
There is no darkness anymore.

That is how life is as well.
Light is always stronger.

Come To Me

Come to me
in pieces
in tiny pieces
torn and worn
beaten
as a complete loser.

Come to me
rejected
misjudged
exhausted.

Come to me!
Get your pieces together
from every corner of the universe
some are dust
some are light
a leaf, a branchlet
whirl and reunite!

Lighthearted Reproach On A Summer Night

Look, I say, the night is crying.
Those are stars, you say.
Once they used to be, I say.
Let me take them as tears.
Don't I have the simple right
to misunderstand
a solid fact like a star?

Between You And Me

Between you and me
there are walls
that we both built over time
slowly
brick by brick.

There are religions
temples
shrines
altars
covenants
word by word.

Between you and me
there are races
white
black
side by side.

There are
all kinds of nasty things
prejudices
fears
doubts
sly laughters
fake smiles

one by one
complexes
type by type.

Between you and me
all these man-made things
are having a wild party
for their
victory over love.

I Am Love

Burn, burn, and burn!
Burn until you become nothing but white ash!
May the winds take the ash away.
May the ash become the dust on a leaf.
May that leaf be given to you with a red rosebud.
May that rosebud blossom in your hands.
May you look carefully at that rose.

Behind the dust, there exists the ash.
Behind the ash, there exists the flame.
I am that flame.
I am that ash.
I am that dust.
I am love.

Octopus

I stood still motionless
in front of a fish stall
at the Tsukiji Fish Market.
The smell of salt, fish, sweat, and blood.

I stood still motionless
all this labor
this greed
these sleepless nights
on moldy boats
on silent boats
all those eyes
watching the sea
of the fishermen who are standing still
motionless
hoping to catch a sign
from the invertebrate.

A body to a soul
is what an octopus is to a human being.
One can taste what it touches
the other can write this poem
never having smelled the salt, fish, sweat, and blood
at a Japanese fish market
never having stood still there, motionless.

Absence

I am drowning in your absence
I am senseless
motionless
my right hand is somewhere
my left hand is somewhere else.
I can't even remember
where I have left my head and feet.

What if you're gone forever?

Manifestation Of Love

I want to dissolve
in the beauty of loving you.

Why can't I just sit under a tree
and watch the world?

Then for no reason at all
why can't I just get up
like a huge mountain
walk to you
then just collapse
the moment I see you?

Can't flowers
of amazing colors
and of heavenly smells
just open up
in front of you
from my ruins?

Can't ivies just grow out of me
grab your feet
climb up around your body
to fix you to me
in case despite such manifestation of love
you still want to turn back and go?

Foggy Road

Isn't this a foggy road that we all drive along?
Monsters of the night hide in the dark to horrify you.

Some tears in a driving-crying mood.
Some speeding first
then a "let them all overtake me" kind of easygoingness.
Some staring at green pastures lying calm on both sides.
Some reproaching to the one sitting next to you
and wondering why they sit and you drive!
Some resentment that the road is harsh
and you are so very tired.

A lot of missing the ones
who left you alone on this foggy road trip.
A lot of glancing back at the road you left behind.
A lot of dreaming about the road ahead.
A lot of worrying to kill that sweet sweet dreaming.

What a unique thing this foggy road is.
It makes you mad sometimes
sometimes hopeful, other times miserable
It has so far made you everything
a sinner, a believer
a toddler, a child, a teenager
a parent hater then a parent.

It makes you love this road.
It makes you hate this road.
It makes you want to pull over
it makes you want to crash!

You start questioning everything about this road
the longness of this road
the shortness of this road
the source of this road
the destination of this road
and every now and then the existence of this road.

This foggy road has something unique
which appeals to a human being
but mostly to our persistence
which constantly shouts at us —
You must keep on driving!

Power

Look at your legs
your feet, your ankles, calves, knees, and thighs.
Do you think
they are the things
which carry you
from day to night
from night to day?

Put your hand on your chest
feel that pounding heart beat.
Do you think
that muscle is the thing
which carries you
from day to night
from night to day?

Hope is all you need!

Teardrop

How small is a teardrop
that
everything fits in it.

How big was this world
still we
two doves
couldn't find a place
to cuddle.

Ocean

Tears are salty drops of water
drops of water just like
the salty waters of the oceans.
When you cry you see tears
yet I see the ocean in you.

Butterflies And Doves

My heart is beating wild
but silent.
I don't want to scare away
the butterflies in my stomach
or the doves sitting on our shoulders.

Soul Whisperer

I am a soul whisperer.
I whisper love to souls.

I do not whisper them visions to look at
I whisper them visions to pass through.

Ask The Fish

You believe
I am closer to other people.
I am indeed
but I am nearest to you.

Even between
two nearest things
there is some kind of a distance.

That's why
I can't name it being nearest.
I can call us
two streams
pouring into the same ocean.

Ask the fish swimming in us:
Where is you?
Where is me?

The Moon

The moon gets big
but is it bigger than my sorrow?

A wise man must have said
loneliness is bearable in the daytime
but a torture at night.

The moon gets bigger
as if a monster is approaching
with its mouth wide open
ready to swallow all those who are lonely at night.

A Game Of Marbles

When I miss you
a child turns up
to play a painful game
somewhere deep in my heart.

The child kneels down
and starts playing a game of marbles.

With no intention to hurt me
he flicks the first marble.
The glass ball rolls and rolls
and then it stops.

His eyes beam with joy.
He glances at the first marble
aims at it
then shoots it with the second.

When I miss you
something little and glass
hits something little and glass in my heart.

I tell the child desperately
It hurts, this game of marbles.
He says —
It's just a game.

Satisfied with this simple answer
I let him play some more.

Deep in me
some little things made of glass
keep hitting
some little things made of glass.

And I miss you more
and more and more.

Dear Traveler

Dear traveler,
I know you have come here to see
the dragonflies living in this lake
but it's mid January
and the lake is frozen.
Ain't no dragonflies in frozen lakes.

Dear lover,
I know you have come here to see
a few tears
but
this heart you adored
has frozen.
Ain't no tears shed by frozen hearts.

I see
you want to stay
you want to put a tent here by the lake
you want to light a fire.
I assume you are doing this to get warmer
not to melt the frozen lake.

Tornado

Let a tornado
destroy
your beliefs
your prejudices
your fears.

Let it sweep away
the past
the future.
Let it demolish
the ancient kingdoms in you
uproot the forests.

Let it drift you away.
Sit back
and watch the twister
mix the colors in you.

Then wake up to a new morning
all peace
all bliss
all forgiveness
all love.

The Echo Of Silence

You sometimes hear a song echoing in your mind
a song you like
or a song you've heard a few times.

What echoes in your existence
when there is silence
the silence after you stop the voice of your ego?

Love Knows No A Little

There is no a little in love.
You cannot love a little
Nor can you say —
I will love you a little.

There is no a little in love.
Can you claim to have swum
when you only
go a little near the lake
sit by it a little
and put your feet up to your knees, a little in water?

You cannot love little by little, either.
Nor can you say, I will love you little by little.
Can you cross a wild flowing river
on a bridge
where you pave the wooden planks
one by one
as you step forward little by little?

There is no a little in love.
Can you convince a child to be a little happy?
The child, when she is happy, is happy to the fullest.

Can you convince a beast to be a little wild?
A beast, when it is hungry, is wild to the fullest.

Love can only be compared to
the happiness of a child
or to the wildness of a beast.
All are to the fullest
none knows a little.

The State Of Love

To be in the state of love is seductive
as it makes you think
life is hiding behind the corner
from where
it will show you
a great face.

This state of being in love is addictive
as it makes you believe
thousands of amazing things
are hiding behind the corner
and will welcome you both
one after another.

The Poppy

I'm tearing apart
the wall of the empty room.

Through the crack in the wall
first only one
then hundreds of red butterflies
fly into the room
beating their wings.

They make me think
poppies are
the vegetal manifestation of these red butterflies
as now I can see the precise tone of red
of these majestically twinkling creatures.

The room is sober gray
and I stand overwhelmed
watching this poppy-red marvel.

Then
I sit down on the floor
and I pull out a wooden floor board.

From the hole in the floor
a spring of water gushes
it knocks down the wall opposite me

and flows free out into the world
to find itself an ocean to pour into.

But everything started
with one single poppy-red butterfly.

The Pounding Beats Of Life

You are just the size of an ant
from the top of a tower.

The size of dust from the moon.

What size is the moon
from within the pupil of your eye
cast in a mirror?

This ant
this tower
this dust
this moon
you
your eye
its pupil
the mirror
and the image reflected in it
beat together.
Listen!

Now take a deep breath
and beat
beat to the pounding beats of life!

The Ponds In Us

A good poem
evokes
the still ponds in us
to flow like wild rivers.

Defining Love

Scarlet
for some people
is a color for their new curtains
matching their new furniture.

Scarlet
for others
is the color of passion.

Water
for some people
is a drink measured in cups.

Water
for others
means oceans to dive.

How can I define love objectively ?
While scarlet, to me
is the color of my love for you
with which I once thought I could paint
the whole afternoon sky.
And while water, to me
was the tears I shed
when I realized
blue had been a better color
for an afternoon sky.

Notorious

I've become the enemy of myself
the maddened lover of you.

How on Earth will I ever dare to touch you?
No one knows
yet
I'm notorious.

Now, you don't talk to me
Neither do I talk to you.

You fall asleep
I hide and watch.

There is no beast big enough
to vomit the pain I have when I'm without you.

I'm dying of jealousy but my hand writes —
I wish you the best of everything.

Clouds pass in the sky
dragging my mind
from every other thing to you.
Then again
and again.

Something that tastes like spring
tries to flee from my mouth
but I keep silent because
I am notorious.

I am my own enemy.
My notoriety has nothing to do
with anything I did to others.

My notoriety comes from
the incredible stories I've been spreading
about how eager I am
to get maddened by love.

Flower Stall

Bright flowers on the corner of the street
red roses and blue irises
are the dream of a beautiful woman
with a pale complexion and thin lips.
Not because she loves red roses or blue irises
but because she needs love.

These same red roses and blue irises
are again the dream of another woman
yet with a darker skin and full lips.
Not because she loves red roses or blue irises
but because she needs money.

One day
the woman with a pale complexion and thin lips
decided to buy herself flowers
and she stopped by the flower stall
of the woman with a dark complexion and full lips.

They looked at each other.
One was jealous of the other's full lips
and the other was jealous of the other's pale skin.
Both failed to appreciate what the other does in life.

But I appreciate these two women
for their courage to survive
not because I have full lips or pale skin
but because they both deserve to be appreciated!

Time And Space

We must first understand
love is the most powerful thing in the universe.

The universe piles up like stacks of white sheets of paper
and time is the binder that keeps those sheets together.

On one page my father is teaching me to ride a bike
on another I'm teaching my child to fly a kite.

All at the same time
as in a book.

There is certainly a God to close this huge book
page by page and all at once.

The Gypsy And The Dervish

There are two odd neighbors
who live next to each other.

One is a daring gypsy woman
with her fluffy white lace skirt
who sings and dances on the streets
fluttering like a sparrow
joyful, idle, and sincere.

The other is a desolate dervish
who hides behind the doors.
With scorn in his eyes
and a worried look
he keeps a careful eye on the gypsy.

Every night, the dervish peers through his curtains
to make sure the gypsy has arrived home safely.

Sometimes the dervish
grabs her arm and stops her from getting on
the first ship to leave the town.
Sometimes the gypsy
puts the head of the dervish on her chest
and sings him a sad tune as he sobs.

They love each other so much
and they tend to hate at times
the two odd neighbors
dwelling side by side
in my head.

Fat Cats

In a neighborhood of old wooden houses
either the birds are weak and thin or the cats.
I never saw a neighborhood with quick strong birds
and fat cats.

You walk up the steep road paved with big stones
up, up, and up.
Then there is a house at the top of the steep road
the house is dark brown wood from outside
the living room has a bay window.
Two dogs live in the front yard.
Here, on summer nights
there is always an old woman sitting at the table.
Stars pass above these houses as the nights go by.
Starry skies flow above these houses as the years go by.
That old woman usually drinks tea
but sometimes she doesn't.
If she doesn't
she must have had a fight with her grandson
or her daughter-in-law
but not with her son.
If she has a fight with her son
she doesn't go down to the garden
she just lies sick in her bed in her room.
They give bread dipped in warm water to the dogs
or the rest of dinner
or just bones.

In a house whose back stands tall over the top of a hill
people grow feelings
then they grow out of them.
They look at the road through the windows
they rush up and down the stairs
they stop on the stairs
they sit on the stairs.

Despite the peeling of paint from the walls
there sits a constant fog on the lives in these houses.
There is always dust on the furniture
first the smell of dust
then white soap
then purple flowers
on top of it the smell of coffee
and on the very top of everything
the sour smell of the wood of the ceiling.
This smell sinks into the bedsheets
the carpets
the people.

Except for the loud green and bright yellow of canaries
the deep purple and the scarlet velvet of the violets
and the jet black suit of the young man
the entire house looks old beige
tired gray
and the walls are dirty white.
The white is a bit gray
the gray is a bit beige
the beige is a bit pale.

The front yards are always wet in the evenings
the dense smell of the watered grapevines
the smell of wet soil that cleanses the soul.

And what if it has rained?
And the rainwater drains down the vines
and what if it soaks the reed-stuffed hard pillows
and what if the color of the pillow-cloth changes?
And what if, inside its beige and gray
little flowers blossom bright
revealing tiny red poppies ?

The guests who come to this house are divided into two
the ones who come down the road
they come exhausted
and mostly bring nothing with them.
The ones who come up the road
they come fresh and happy and they bring many things.
The neighboring women
bring grape-leaf rolls and stuffed peppers
inside cheap aluminum pots
fresh scallions wrapped in old newspapers
and three eggs taken from the hens that morning.
But mostly they bring
grape-leaf rolls and stuffed peppers.

At night
the beloved son of the old woman
the husband of the woman
the father of the young man with a black suit
brings a bottle of raki
wrapped in an old newspaper
and concealed in a black plastic bag.
The young man brings the books
he buys and reads the first half during his lunch break
and the rest on the bus on the way back home.

And you can leave these houses in two different ways
one is by walking down the road
as your toes hit the front of your shoes
the other way is by walking up the road
as your heels hit the back of your shoes.

No meaning is given to the wood
the red sunset
or the draining of rainwater from vines.
Then one day
a stranger comes to this house
she stays in this house for a while
she sits on the stairs in this house
the young man reads her a poem on the stairs
they hold hands
they walk down the road
they walk up the road.

Every meaning dashes to them on these stairs
and becomes a lump in their throats
and they hardly swallow what they feel.
Now the house is unforgettable
together with the people in this house
and the purple violets, and the stairs.

Because these houses are enchanting
and the people in them, too.
Those young men in black suits
and young girls who give a meaning to everything.
If we stop here, our short story will be a poem
if we write an ending, it will be a short story.
But either way it will be a piece of literature
because when two different lives
from two different parts of a town intersect
there is love.
If there is no love, these two lives hardly intersect.

The life in downtown flashes like a stream of light
yellow and red.
People who know each other
kiss each other cheek to cheek
they step out of warm cars
they walk into the hallways of warm apartment blocks
this is how the story goes on in a city.
Then suddenly the invisible becomes visible
and you start seeing the wooden houses
where time moves at a slower pace.

You start seeing the gray rooms
and you understand holding hands
is very practical on steep stone-paved roads.
However, it doesn't last for a long time.
The love story ends.
Everyone goes back to their bedrooms
to their homes
to their streets
to wherever they belong.
To familiar faces, familiar sounds.
You have noone who startles you.
The fairy tale has ended.

The young man in a suit is fine
not because he isn't sad about it
but because he is accustomed to being sad about things.
He grew up too early.
But the girl hasn't grown up yet.
She has never accepted these kinds of endings
she never went with the flow.
And if the girl is a poet
every night for the next twenty years
she will be missing that house.
It must be that
the last footsteps are heard in the street
then the door has closed crackling.
The gold dog is sleeping under the vines.
The big black one is on the right of the gate.
The stairs are empty and dark.

Yoga Narasimha Swamy Temple, Melukote, India

Close to my heart
far in the distance
as close as a blink of an eye
as far as a continent
an image frozen.

An image frozen with leaves rustling
bees flying
soil breathing.

The frozen image inhales me
breathes out my body
keeps in my soul.

Déjà Vu

Although there are very convincing
scientific explanations
about what déjà vu is,
still
each time
I happen to find myself
thinking —
Back to the default mode? Again?

In The Night Garden

In the night garden
I don't think plants sleep at night.
Some maybe, but not all, I'm sure.
On top of a thin body
from within the void among their petals
they are moon bathing.
Purple hyacinths are like little children
who giggle and murmur
and giggle again
until they fall asleep.

The Habit

How can one love this much ?

This is a pinkish redness of the coming evening
then some parliament blue, and finally some purple.
Step by step, the sunshine walks away.
The right side of your face is still in light.

Have you glanced at the door?
Perhaps I was mistaken.
Are you expecting someone?
Maybe you want to get up and leave
as somewhere someone else is expecting you?

How on earth did you get the charming habit
of being shy when smiling?

The Best Part

I wasn't born with you.
It seems to me that
I won't be able to die in your company.

Still however,
you were the very best part
between the introduction and the conclusion.

The Ganges

In the early morning, mist covered me.
You didn't show up.

I waited for you under the midday sun.
You didn't come then, either.

With the hope of seeing you
I searched my banks.
I looked at each and every face in my waters
I searched for you in the crowds.

And now the moon is shining on me
even the Sadhus have left.
With my thousands of candle eyes
with flower petals in my heart
I'm still waiting for you.

I am never alone, you know.
I am never alone
still I feel lonely.

Lovers At Night

Slowly
put your head
on my chest!

Take off your worries
strip your soul
from this world!

I'm about to row the boat
towards us.

Come, join me
in this peaceful ride!

Soul

My God is such an artist
an artist to create something so unbelievable
that the loving one
wrapped it with something less unbelievable.

A human being is
the amazing package of soul.

A Sweet Dream

I want to wake up to a dream
a dream sweet enough
to make me forget
the bitter taste of reality.

Vain Effort

Every night this beast comes here
puts his sharp yellow teeth
on my flesh
and eats my heart alive.

Only when the night is over
I get some sleep.

It's a curse for lovers
to try to forget.

A vain effort to fight back against a beast
with blood dripping yellow teeth.

Things Fall Apart

There is nothing more to hide
'cause things fall apart.
Things fall apart.

Seldom I feared someone.
Mostly I trusted them.
I hardly ever hurt
or never meant to hurt anyone.
But now things fall apart.
In the end I fall apart.

The sugar building where I hide
is about to collapse
together with everything I've designed
'cause things fall apart.
Things fall apart.

Love is the name for God.
Patience is the way I've walked.
But you have to know, my dear
things fall apart.
Things fall apart.

Step by step I've become who I am.
With tears I've paid for my mistakes
so now I have no regrets.

Then it starts to rain.
Again I'm all alone within my sweet pain.
Then all of a sudden
things fall apart.
Things fall apart.

They must make a statue of me crucified on a cross.
They must crown my head with a halo.
My figurine, with a thousand arms
must be placed in a temple
not for my compassion
my pureness
or my call for salvation
but for my invincible belief in love.

Some lost their friends in the walk of life
some lost their fame
some got a very bad name.
I traded everything for love.
Hold on tight!
'Cause things fall apart.
Things
fall
apart.

I Am Proud Of My Heart

I am proud of my heart.
It has been played
stabbed, cheated
burned and broken.
But somehow
it still works.

Ships Are Crossing Across My Heart

Ships are crossing across my heart
not in water
but in flesh.

They are passing
ripping my heart deep in flesh
blood and pain.

A colossal fleet of glass vessels
is trying to move
tears, blood, and pain.

My heart is breaking
breaking pieces into pieces.

Another night of loneliness
where the ships set sail on a quest for your hollow ghost
towards the horizon
the horizon of a whole red loneliness.

Union

Once a river
meets the ocean
can it flow backwards
and forget meeting the ocean?

Agony

In the shabby house with two storeys
the hands of the unknown present
have just stabbed the past.

It is dying in the same room with me.
Disgustingly, the darkest of all bloods
flows on the floor next to my feet.

We are dying like two strangers
with no empathy for each other
both trying to survive
in such great pain.

My head is half frozen.
My hands are cut off.

I am no one.
I own no past.
I owe nothing to the future tonight
even the agony is gently dying.

Flowers Of Fire

The dervishes are whirling
like flowers of fire blossoming in darkness
like stars spread in the universe
like a breath whispering — Allah!

On This Night Of Separation

On this night of separation
remember yourself always as I always remember you!

Now please dig a very deep grave
let me get closer to the edge
let me hang my arm down into it
and all those incredibly beautiful days
and nights
all the feelings I have for you
and the brightness in my eyes when I think of you
the skimming stones in my heart
when I hear your name.
Through my fingertips
all these things fall into the deep grave
after they are peeled off my being
as flesh getting skinned from the bones.

Or else, on this night of separation
how am I supposed to walk away from out of us?

The Blossom Of A Soul

The blossom of a soul
is in a smile.

When some people smile
that smile
runs towards you
like a healthy child who runs
in the meadows towards you
holding a golden stem of wheat.

You just want to open your arms wide.

The Eagle Ate The Truth

How sweet this desire is!
How strong the eagle is!
How hard it is
not to break under our obligations.

Lots of things pulled me back
from this sweet desire.
Yet the eagle ate the truth
and he devoured my common sense, too.

As yet, I haven't lost my reason to say
the sky is blue because of you
but I know for sure
you are my reason for gazing at that blue.

Happy Birthday

The seed under the soil grows up
shoots grow first
then a tree
then the fruits.
Let's think of an orange.

There are seeds in the orange, too.
Now let me ask you, my friend
are you the seed under the soil
the shoots
the tree
the orange
or the seeds inside the orange?

You are growing, my friend, you are growing.

To me, you are all of them.
You are also the morning breeze in the orange grove
blowing gently
among the trees.

The Redness Of Dusk

The redness of dusk
has painted a dusty main road
in this town in the midwest.
Among figures of Jesus and Mary
and the pastel shades of the patchworks
she stood up
walked out of the small store
to the middle of the empty road
paused there
and faced the setting sun
with her legs apart.
She watched the breathtaking redness of the sky
under the setting sun
the parked cars
the main street
together with
the front walls and windows of the shops
shining bright with a red glaze
as if she was expecting a sign
to give her some courage
not to
walk back into the store
behind the cash register
surrounded by figures of Jesus and Mary
across from the piles of folded pastel patchwork quilts.

Ugly Black

Where have all the colors gone?
I thought they were dancing in water
suddenly
the black fish swallowed them all greedily
it sent all my colors to its stomach
where the shattered pieces of my heart are crackling.

The Dress

Once I loved a man in the land of colors and spice.
Now I am far beyond blue, orange, and dark pink
now I am far beyond the smells of turmeric and saffron.
I am far beyond the land I wished to visit
the dress I wished to wear.
Once I loved you, now I am far beyond you, me, and us.

I am far beyond myself.
I am far beyond this world.
Once I was tied to you with the invisible ropes of hope
now I am far beyond.

Your ugly words broke the spell
cut the ropes, terrified my hope.

The Night

The night has come
as always
without asking.

What great company
silent, silent, silent.

The night knows how to listen!

On Crimson Sunsets

The hearts of lovers
are burned with
a scarlet seal.

That's why
they long for each other far more
on crimson sunsets.

When You Leave Me

When you leave me
I feel as if
I'm standing
in the crowds
when suddenly
everyone turns their backs to me
and walks out on me.

I can't even cope with a single parting from you.
How will I ever survive all these partings?

When you leave me
I feel as if
you walk out on me in hundreds
each you
dragging a joy
a color
a piece of my poor heart.

Weaving Myself A Crown

A friend of mine asked me —
What have you been doing?
Nothing much, I replied,
except for
weaving myself a crown
weaving all together
a word of him
a moment with him
and what I've become with him.

I was so immersed in this weaving that
I happened to braid together
my fingers
my hands
my arms
my soul.

September

When you left me
you rode away stealing the spring
and left me with nothing but too ugly falls.

Falls are not good for romantics
if the red leaves are red red leaves.

Caged Bird

My birds aren't caged.
My dolphins aren't familiar with tanks or nets.
My beasts are bulletproof.

Just like love
they know no fear
no limits
no limitations.

Tentacles Of Night
(To my daughter)

The tentacles of night reach out for me.
They touch my cold hands
my frozen face
my half body.

When you aren't here with me
the tentacles of night reach out for me.

The Bridge To Nowhere

There was no one on the bridge to nowhere.
Neither on this side of nowhere, nor on the other.
I'd walked all the way up to the bridge to nowhere.
However
stepping on the worn wood
I changed my mind
and I turned back.

A Pause In The Flow

Two strangers are walking towards each other.
Suddenly, pausing, they look at each other.
And the wild mustangs
galloping just a few seconds ago
also pause
scared to make
the two strangers
turn their backs
and walk away.

You Must Love Me

Not because
I must be loved
or
you must love
but
you must love me.

Outlander

The sky has become a bizarre red.
I, myself have also become a bizarre color.
Now I am an outlander.

You say to me —
You are at home.
Sadly, I utter —
I am an outlander in my own self.

Twisted

When a love fails
your soul is twisted
your heart is twisted
your smiles are twisted.

You sit in crowds
like a piece of furniture
inherited from your grandparents
faded
old
and odd
in a living room
full of brand new furniture.

Don't worry.
After some time
you will surely find the right place for yourself
like that piece of furniture will find the right place
in the living room.

Blue Mouth

When you give up on somebody
your mouth turns blue.

You try hard to say something nice
with that blue mouth getting colder.

The harder you try
the more blue the mouth gets
the colder the heart gets.

Some time later
the blue mouth quits talking.

The couple surrenders to silence
the silence of two blue mouths
two frozen hearts.

It Rains On You

It rains on you.
I watch water drops fall on you.
They soak my heart.
My heart fills up with rain water.
Then out of the blue
you ask me —
Do you love me?

Sorting Out Things

Sorting out the things I have
I kept you
abandoned everything else.

Night And Longing

The night has come to visit me
together with longing
another good old friend.

I asked about you to the night
she didn't know you.

I asked about you to the longing
she knew nothing but you.

Longing left early, promising to send you back to me.
As she walked gracefully away
I could barely whisper —
Please!

Red

Red as a burning fire on top of a mountain at night.
Red as a single poppy in a vast green pasture.
Red in the heart, a burning passion.
Red as a red rose, a whirling child of Adam.

Giant Sharks

I sometimes wish
we had giant sharks
with sharp and scary teeth
always hungry and ready to eat
anyone we throw at them like bait.
Such as the bad guys
whom we believe are the reason
for the hunger of the hungry children
and all evil deeds.

Then
who will judge
the sharks
the sharp teeth
and our deeds?

Sunset

In the past
when I sat to watch the sunset
I could see nothing but some sad memories
that dash like a seam of clouds
towards the purple and scarlet horizon
stepping on my tired shoulders
and then on my troubled head.

Now
I'm sitting at the same spot again
to watch the sunset
but this time
in peace
in forgiveness
in awareness.

I cannot make what I see fit
neither in my small eyes
nor in my finest words.

Divine Embrace

There is something horribly frantic
about the way we think —
I am one thing, you are another thing.

In fact, there is one thing
a whole one being
a network of cords
like veins in a human being
like branches of a tree
like galaxies scattered in the universes
we whirl and whirl and whirl
within that oneness
into that oneness.

Time is the nicest blanket covering
this magnificent embrace.

Silence Of Love

My eyes are craving for your eyes
but more than anything
they are craving for the silence
when you close your eyes
and the darkness
when I close mine.

Skylark

Love is a burning fire
a twisting tornado of blazing fire.
It burns and burns.
It hurts and hurts.
It maddens my heart, devastates my soul.

If you see a skylark
flying straight to that fire
call that skylark a lover.
Or else do not waste that sweet word.

You Are In Love

Love is visible on your face
from a "don't know why" kind of smile
from a "whatever" twist of your lips
from a "don't know for how long" gaze at the clouds.

When I'm Gone

When I'm gone, dearest
don't ever be sad
try to smile instead.

Smile
like a devoted gardener
who smiles at the rose hips
or at the carnations
or at his muddy boots.

Index of Poems by Titles

About the Poet Peacef Pya

The Turkish poet Peacef Pya writes fluently in two languages: Turkish and English. She studied translation and interpretation in three languages (Turkish, English and French), and she has an M.A. in teaching English. For fifteen years, Pya has been teaching English at a leading university in Turkey. Currently, she is editing her second book of poems.

Entangling: Poems by Peacef Pya is a garden of timeless poems about the beauties, the mysteries, and the struggles within the human heart and soul. Each of the book's 108 poems is a unique gem, radiant with wonder and delight. The captured moments are memorable, the images are striking, the language is direct and fresh. Pya believes that poetry heals wounds, and poets whisper to fallen birds to tell them, "You can fly!" Poems nourish the human soul, nestle on the twisted corner of the lips of lovers, and make the frozen waters of a human heart rush like powerful waterfalls and then plunge into oceans of hope and love.

About Zorba Press

Zorba Press is an independent publisher of books, ebooks, and audio books. From the gorgeous gorges of Ithaca, New York, we publish **The Zorba Anthology of Love Stories; The Ithaca Manual of Style;** the anthology **Zenlightenment;** and a wild novel about love and eros (for adults) **Thoreau Bound: A Utopian Romance in the Isles of Greece.**

Currently, we offer about 30 titles – fiction and non-fiction – and we are eager to build our list with quality authors and books. Our recent publications include **Entangling: Poems by Peacef Pya; My Life on the Ragged Paths of Pan: Selected Poems and Translations by Thanasis Maskaleris;** and paperback and ebook editions of a modern classic, Michael Tobias's extraordinary 625,000-word novel, **The Adventures of Mr Marigold.**

Zorba's mission is to promote the innovative ideas and the daring books that nourish children and childhood, point the way to a culture of non-violence, create a sustainable future, and nurture — for every living being — a new world of love, kindness, courage, creativity, sincerity, and peace.

Visit Zorba Press at www.ZorbaPress.com

www.ingramcontent.com/pod-product-compliance
Lightning Source LLC
Chambersburg PA
CBHW051729040426
42447CB00008B/1037